SUNFLOWER SEEDS

SUNFLOWER SEEDS

· · ·

SONIA SUMMER

ISBN: 979-8-9864575-0-5

Library of Congress Control Number: 2022914816

Cover Design by Nuno Moreira
Interior Design and Editing by Sonia Summer

Printed in the United States of America

· *love letters* ·

FOR JORDAN— I've been writing you letters and poems since we were kids. this dedication only helps to keep the tradition going. even into adulthood, you are still my safest place. thank you for reminding me to pick up my pen. for daring me to walk to the sun with you. although it is scalding, you will never be alone. together we cleanse in the crucible of our adversities. together we emerge celestial and gold.

FOR ALL OF MY PEOPLE OF COLOR— whether bruised or untouched. I may not know each of your names, but I know your skeletons very well. have you never heard of compost? we can rise renewed from anything.

· CONTENTS ·

one.

IN FIELD / FROM YAAD

(warriors born into revolution)

· SUNFLOWER SEED ·

My son,
I devour your smell through cord
and rough
and roof
and swelling.
you have made home of this single dwelling
singlehandedly shifting and stealing space from organs—
already stealing hearts from their owners.
you are the most sweet, smooth,
stubborn tale of grand larceny.

our harmony:

    do you feel me breathing through your nose,
    my voice humming in your throat?
    mommy is here.

and as you wade
the depths
the oceans
the seas of me
(praised by your father
and consecrated by our other),
you will surely understand how vast
I have become
to accommodate our love.

· SUBTLE AND BRIEF ·

Lately you are all my hands talk about
and they (all of them)
are wondering
(inquiring)
when you will release my breath
you clench onto so dearly—
gripping my awe like matter.

I look at you
you look into me
in the quiet of ours
subtle and brief.

I've had a terrible time
trying to resist your newborn body heat
trying not to melt into you
but as you learn
to take mama's hand,
I remember what presence
should feel like
and everything
I once thought I was
dissolves in the presence
of who you are.

we deserve each other.

I dreamt of who you were
with no expectation
of who you will become
other than alive and full of life
with a life full of its
traditional ebbs and flows.

I look into you
you look at me
in the quiet of ours
subtle and brief.

wherever you go,
I will follow
with all of my hands
to catch, to teach,
to hold, to be taught.
we will wrought like iron
welded into one fold
in the quiet for hours,
not so subtly,
for a lifetime.

· AMERICA, THE DYING ·

Seeded black woman,
please accept america's apology
on my behalf.

she is dying and your black son
was blooming so sweet
like humming hyssop
in your bellowing pyramid;
as though he was destined to cleanse plague
from this earth with his words.

but as you must know
at least every two-fifths of you
must pay an expense.
and if I am being honest
you were in such awe of his future,
she simply could not stand
the stench
of his purpose.

from what I am told
she just wasn't expecting it—
for you to bring marigold into her funeral.

· FEAR THE COLORED AND INNOCENT ·

He was black
and grown ass man

                                        (tall child)

hooded
and anonymous

                                        (therefore 'sinister'
                                        and 'up to no good')

it was only right
the cops took to hip hop
and spit a sweet sixteen in him
but the words went right through 'em
dumb n****r
then they prodded him
with sticks
in fear he may still be

                                        (moving)
                                        (alive)

a threat.

                                        because it takes
                                        sixteen to sixty
                                        silver bullets now!

                                        we are so superhuman—
                                        so scary now!

· POLITICALLY INCORRECT ·

You cannot tell a mother that her son is dead
before he has ever lived
then fluster all upset
when she asks
'why'

as if eight years of obama
is supposed to humble her
from mourning

wasn't it eight months of bush
that had america saying
'never forget'

why is it that only everything you say matters?

· LIFE INTERRUPTED ·

Melted wax on birthday cake
he would have been teen today
the colored folk genocide is now legalized

legal now! legal now!
colored folk for grabs
it is legal now!

(not that you needed the paperwork)

in voting booth
in jail cell
in class
in court

in group chats
circulating high schools
or in drive thrus
like drive-bys on playgrounds on record

in the middle of the night
in silence
in apartments you don't belong
right building wrong person
or when all intel is just wrong

at work
at supermarket
at first glance
without a thought
on television
on live stream
on phone
at traffic stop

in the words of the late june jordan:

> *tell me something*
> *what you think would happen if*
> *every time they kill a black boy*
> *then we kill a cop*
> *every time they kill a black man*
> *then we kill a cop*

> *you think the accident rate would lower subsequently?*

tell me something
is our quality of life intended to be supplementary?
does human decency only come in white sold separately?

(a special thank you in advance if these words do not apply)

at gas station
at board meeting
on foot
on bike
on paper
with a paper trail of cookies online

we are running out of space
so we create
multiple t-shirts
to fit all the names
we are over the dedications
the conversations leading to no change
we've left our expectations vacant
and moved away from the high rent
'cause it's only the first of the month
and the first nine have already died

how high of a price do you want us to pay?

we are tired of risking life
over hoodie
and pizza
and protest
and park walk

being harassed
on train
and airplane
by vote
by zip code
we have been moved
like cargo
from our homes
to outlines
on sidewalk
we are cheap chalk
on everything
turn off the street lights
bring out the torches
we let the pot simmer
but now we're broiling

LAW ENFORCEMENT NEEDS TO COME WITH A TRIGGER WARNING

do y'all ever review your body cam footage
and take a look at yourselves?
matter fact
maybe that is the issue
you are too consumed with looking at yourselves
looking through your point of view

like you're playing a game
like you're playing survivor
like we didn't call you
like we are the monsters

even at traffic stops
every time you get triggered we get shot
when we are in danger we hesitate to call
you either do too much or nothing at all

meanwhile we are taken to coroner in handcuffs
still a threat although still unarmed
leaving our families broken and devastated
leaving our bodies faceless and obliterated
we are not nameless
it's just a lot of us to remember
hesitant to make a list 'cause I don't want to forget one
and I don't want to have to add one
after the list is already published
but it's hard
'cause I want to acknowledge
all the lives we have lost
the justice that went uncrossed
CONGRATS
you took the short way to still make it home
but at what cost

· AMERICA, THE BEAUTIFUL ·

Preparing for dinner she puts on her pearls
america: harbors of soot
wonder where she harbors her drinking water

guilty is the one
who washes their hands
first after war

where is the justice
lit torches
cold pangs of pitch forks
against china
so many walls
of their china

her daughters cry in dumpsters
not paralyzed
but in a trance
this garbage feels like womb
but less corrupt than mommy
carbon copy?

daddy says bless america
mommy's blessed
mommy
is blessed

she chimneys through harbors
of soot like santa
baiting you to be good
as she scrubs
underneath her nail beds
just in time for dinner

on grill
working pork chops
for the fourth
passing overseas bills for another trill
that no one can afford
while over a fourth hold
open mouths
crowded appetites
and flustered pockets

no, no,
never in america

dinner is always made
dinner is always done
dinner is always served

it is just
invitation only

· ARTIFICIAL FREEDOM *(WHEN PLANTS NEED SOIL BUT ONLY HAVE HOUSES)* ·

The brickhouse suffocated grandpa.
he didn't stand a chance.
he gasped for water,
he stretched for sun,
but still died in mama's hands.

the whitehouse suffocated grandpa.
we hunted desperately for an escape.
poor papa,
papa gone.
mama went insane.

the greenhouse yearned for grandpa.
the fields were thick and dense.
he'd fought for acres,
for decades,
and got white picket fence.

it seemed right to forget
the flowers that winter.
we released him to the sun:
he burned on cinder.

· BREACHING BORDERS ·

I am no place for crowds and yet all these men
are stationed inside me like barracks.
they say these men are my indigenous people
and I must carry them to every war.

they are:
unruly, resistant, fresh, clever.

dissatisfied with:
bending backward, less and shackle.

unknowingly, I've made fools of them (these men)
allowing others who've made fools of me
to breach my borders as if these warriors
have not breached my flesh
and made home of my blood.

ancestry isn't the kind of thing you can wash out;
this is not the kind of blood that can be rung from fibers.

it smells like sundown.
it cleanses like fire.

it stains a person.

· FOR THE WOMAN LINED IN PROGRESS ·

I will not be ashamed of my stretch marks;
they're like a scrolling marquee across my waistline
through my stomach, thighs, breasts and ass
that scream, sigh and whisper
roasted redwood with butternut blush
and a splash
of mocha muscle.

it's just something about the s t r e t c h
how it marks the pinnacle of being
and flavor
and depth
and strength
and woman in me.

the sweetest scars my body could've ever kept
line me and punctuate my stories
(they pull me to the side and fill me).

they are waves in my river keeping me current;
they dictate the skin I once filled
before it got spread open—
'cause I needed more space to exist, erupt and breathe.

my body needed to become more in order to contain me.

I am supernatural,
heavyweight volcano,
jamaican taino, maroon.
my body has to make room
for the warriors inside of me
for 1738
for the mountains
tectonic plates
for the weight.
and my eruption is more than worth the wait.

my body is roiling with heat.
she's royal, yeah, so royal and—
and I'm already riled up so please
don't let me learn any more of my ancestry.
I might have to go mount kilimanjaro
an' kill a man who wan' war wit me!

I will not be ashamed of my stretch marks
and how they lay and demarcate
the boundaries I've left behind
and the boundaries I've reinforced.
they are a force—
I am a force—
to be reckoned with.

· MELANIN ·

We are the mitochondria of nations
a lethal powerhouse in 'highbrow and sagacious'
on the outskirts of 'needing your approval'
which is far from 'pick me'
just please
leave me alone to blossom in the land
my ancestors chose

I am an alchemist with the prose
steady making statements like
'no matter how we are posed—
ghetto fabulous *is* high fashion'
we are all natural, cage free black
renaissance men and women
our bodies will decompose if you do not tend to us

you ask us
are we not self sufficient
sounds like you're fishing for an alley-oop setup
would you prefer we expect nothing from you at all?
plot twist— we never did

can the colonizer hills get any *steeper*
can the crowd be any more *stiff*
someone please make the audience *great again*
someone please *defund the FBI*

mouth on ignorant
melanin on immigrant
scent on hibiscus
callaloo and saltfish for breakfast
my soul is thicker than the harry potter books on my bookshelf
my baby hair's unruly
but sometimes it's slicked with sweat
from carrying this conversation all by myself
from carrying *these bags* all by myself
from carrying *this ass* all by myself
(come on, you knew that was coming)
but this is not a welcome letter
for unsolicited and unwarranted comments
for soliciting outside our houses to do unwarranted raids
oh, too soon?
for who?
you?
riiiiight.

this is also not a welcome letter for crocodile tear solicitude
the type that's poorly timed and never matches the words
the kind that's always a day late and a dollar short
the one that tries to paint you a picture of how your people are a nuisance
but you ain't no bob ross we can see through your forest
and all your happy trees
have nooses

· BLACK WOMAN— PLEASE REGARD THE BLACK ·

If you are upset that you bought this book
and it is already saying horrendous things
like black instead of brown
(because 'brown' is more polite)
then you do not love me.
you love to nazi (not see) all of me
in fear I may become more relatable to you.
you only agree with the parts of me
that you can screenshot, mood board and profit off.

you will say I am a threat.
that I am not mainstream friendly 'cause I politic incorrect.
that I am not the cute lil' poet you thought you were gonna get.
but you just can not
tiptoe
over
my skin
without
inciting flame.
and before you jump to any conclusions
about this matchstick of a woman,
I am equally heavy on moisture as I am artillery
so feel free to aim all the hoses at me
'cause, baby,
I am still fire when wet.

· DELAYED PROLOGUE ·

I am your favorite kind of story:
crashing, porous, hard to swallow,
gritty, unforgettable and ever-shifting;
a mix between autobiography and museum
so don't go skipping through me— that's just ill-mannered.
I am a stunning kahlo, a time capsule memorial.
word to frida, you're free to appreciate my art
but you're gonna relish in my beauty
at the same damn time.
because you are the century I may never see
but wish to be a part of forever
and whosoever doubts me
speak now or forever hold your peace
'cause best believe I'm holding mine.
I bit through brick and glass
to find my voice for a moment like this
and still manage to smile;
bloody but breathing— demanding my respect;
salivating and seething, I'm not teething
I just want my lick back.
but my God says he got me so I just sit back,
forgive, release and pray.
I'm a queen around queens
and I know you're hungry for more.
although slightly delayed,
this is the prologue.

two.

AT BODEGA

(growing pains and the unforgiving frost)

· THE LOCAL GIRLS ·

We all knew next year would be much different
til' then everything was cool

double dutch double dutch baker's man
left hand left hand left foot in

we all washed the playgrounds with our
sweat beads and some of us
began dropping off our innocence
through hints in pencil grooves
on schoolboy desks

feet on cracks
breaking backs
like old times

we all snatched soul and homes
through phone lines in our notebooks
and last-day-of-school disposable cameras
unaware of any (and all) danger
young and eager to be familiar
with straight hair
and brow waxes
and shy glances
and nine periods a day
and one period a month

and boo lovin'
and homegirl parties
and first kisses (do it right)
and last dance of the night (get it done)
and field tripping
and boy tripping
and "my girl's trippin'"
not to mention corner store fights
and call me but—
only after 9
'cause I want to pay attention
but don't want to pay
for minutes
not even for a second
matter fact hit me back
at 9:01
just to be safe

we all were impatient to get life started
yet full of complaints as soon as it got going

adolescence sauntered over like it had
just what we wanted
even if
but for a moment

· RED MATTER ·

For the sissy who gets queasy about periods:
tell me what is so defiling about my womb
recycling itself
and why do you find relief
in the censorship of its habitual birth?

allow me the space
to be vulnerable,
to feed myself,
to bleed and mourn the moon.

my body assassinates monthly.

the least you could do is let me
incinerate in comfort
and riot in peace.

· ROOTS ·

A girl incubates in the palms of her father.
living for his pride, she may lose balance
but remains adamant in finding her way
through his shoes.
lost in his views,
little girl,
your feet will only melt
in the heels of his footprints.

instead be yourself.

make your mistakes.

remember his advice:
think and swallow twice
to keep your spine from ejecting
just to be entwined in another's web
resembling protection;
only let your body slump for those
who have temporary backbones to lend you and
never forget the footsteps your father took
to uproot earth and ground you.

· JANE FOOLERY ·

Summer is coming.

don't be the heart orphaned
on yellow brick road
with long legs and unkempt soul.

children never find dinner
whilst searching for hopscotch.

· FIREFLOWER ·

When school was out,
we had recess at the park.
fresh boys played booty tag.
fresh girls got caught.

with permed roots and no promiscuous edges,
I cooled my nerves with shaved ice and a swing.
I suppose this was the awkward age
between wanting to be seen
but still
not wanting to be touched.

until then,
I crossed the park alongside court
journeying through
wildebeests dirty dancing in field
to take my ass home before track practice.

my school friend stayed
laid on weeds and grass (mostly weeds)
like foreign flower in her own garden
plucked too soon
(columbus boys will do that to you—
stumble upon your sap then try to god your body
like they created something knowing
it was already there before them).

said school friend and her friend
laid in sweat from sin and sun.
(his) hand down (her) pants
with all clouds watching and she looked upon them
squinting as they turned to abstract
and blot.

her cheeks burned red
not for the slight red tint
on his skin
but for the switches
in his fingers
and the wildfire he ignited
inside her.

and honey,
between you and me,
the vegetation was scalding.

· DRIVE-BY CATCALLS ·

Scoop me up a lil' love pint of that thang
come back to my place let's shoot the breeze and cool it
I like a bitch who's a bit thick and soft-served
tasteful and easily spread
yo thang has me musing to pac's "what'z ya phone #"
that *nasty!* the things I'm gon' do to you girl
you so sweet and all unprocessed and organic and shit
you got what I want so what I gotta say to make you stop
damn it moves like water when you walk! see, that's that *thang!*

    just keep walking   maybe I should turn around
        you know what fuck it

            scoop me up a bit of your nerve
            to have reimagined me as melted banana split sundae
            all that sight wasted— eyes wide and seein' nothin'
            filled with know-better and know-how
            but talkin' like street-beast just 'cause I'm walking past
            and ya lil' dick jumped so you jumpin'
            to conclusions and lustin' over me
            I promise nothing's more unattractive
            than watching you beg for a nut
            ain't nothin' easy 'bout me mister man
            I'm the final boss— you don't get to play with me
            'til you step your game and respect all the way up!
            better act like you know!

· LEFT ON READ ·

Why so delicate
why so wilted
why so heartfelt
why so tender
why so teardrop teardrop
why so crybaby beautiful
why you feel so much
why you not feelin' me
why you always frontin'
why you tryna tie me down
why you not committed
why you so disobedient
why you can't pick up the phone when I have time for you

baby you know I'm like karma
I always come back around

(delivered)
(read)

· PHOTOSYNTHESIS ·

Don't you know sunflowers stretch toward sun?
now tell me— what direction do you see me goin'?

did you expect my petals to settle for artificial heat?
you really thought you could 'truman show' me?

am I not miraculously grown— no miracle gro?
aren't you corsage cut and vase stowed?

why are you asking for explanation from the one with no expiration?
does my glory not meet your street expectation?

is this not exemplary of the product questioning the source?
do you not orbit around me like centripetal force?

you want me to loom in gloom
and compromise nature whenever we disagree,
but who else you know creates in womb
and blooms like beast?

· LADY BLOSSOM ·

I woke up in an uneven veil of your yellow.
found my silhouette distorted
and misshaped in finger paint
and your tainted fingers.
skin colored in your blurry mixture
of yellowed, fall hues.

you were a childish artist.

a childish lover unconcerned
about concepts like:
the feelings of others
and your word.

and yet,
no matter how many
forgotten hues
(the colors you would never
choose to paint me),
I would wake up
saturated in your yellow
grateful to just be painted
thick
in someone.

because I, too, was a childish lover
unconcerned about concepts like:
knowing myself
and self worth;
modest in the subjects of me
yet mastering you.
like a slot machine
waiting to be played with and eager for change,
I wanted your fingers to smudge my browns
and dilute me.

this was the perfect tale of 'be careful what you wish for.'

I woke up grateful to be infused and outlined in you
supposing I'd want to grow yellow and old.
until that moment I fell and ripped the veil,
remembering I am celestial
and gold.

· BIG SISTER ·

But how dare they catch and silence your echoes?
when we're put into the mix
they have to stir us in like molasses
to thicken the batter.

we make it rich.

we are literally gold, do you understand?

the moment you realize how big you are,
no one will ever be able
to stunt your growth again.

· RLTNSHP ·

We were the only fairytale that began with 'eventually'
we couldn't possibly qualify as a love story
we were an abbreviation
like a dedication:

    "here's to the two
    who tried"

we were a sweet session of seconds
with jealous tendencies,
faulty perceptions
and no real chance
at eternity

    "eventually,
    they would realize
    there were no butterflies in their stomachs
    only ulcer-shaped mistakes
    and consequential moments"

we were the definition of curtains closing
a dramatic display
whose ending warranted applause

· HOLY ·

Sometimes we need to open our circles
so people can step out.
open our wombs not only for creation
but to let out waste.

I know you are accustomed to making art
from scraps you've scraped
but not every accumulation creates pearls.

some trash is just trash.

it is simply not biodegradable;
it's unnatural
and just won't sit well with you.
it will sit in your gut
even through your burial
and outlive your skeleton
by centuries.

imagine holding on to hope
(tucking the rope with you in casket)
and five hundred years pass by—
no soul in sight, body decomposed,
and all that's left is the manmade waste
you forced down your throat
that earth knew better than to swallow.

imagine clogging pores with fool's plastic
because it's shimmering and shining,
holding on to litter 'cause it glittered
like diamonds.

baby,
most things glimmer under water
simply because you are standing
above the surface
and are the sun.

· CASTLE FOOLS ·

Queen,
I saw you emerge from the depths of hell
with a crooked crown and limping heart.

your limbs
dangling and strung
with knots of rope and thread.
I heard he used your shadow
because he thought
your beauty was not enough.
it's a shame puppets can't scream.

queen,
how could you let someone
turn you into a jester and clown you?

· HEAR ME OUT ·

I hate when you finally talk to someone
you've been interested in
and you have to hold back
half your essence
and water down whole soul
to keep from overwhelming them.

like, 'but no,
I've dreamt of this all
already,
I promise it went okay.
we can do this.'

that awkward (unfortunate) stage
between visualizing,
manifesting
and just sounding like a stalker.

· SEVENS OF PETALS ·

I walked to your home with a pocketful of picked petals
grazing the lint-licked lining of my jeans
(pre-counted to assure 'she loves me')
and I'm hoping you love me
love me too

sevens of petals in my pockets

    knock knock knot

knots today
stomach in knots today

    knock knock

I'm here with
sevens of petals in my pockets
and sevens of second haiku lines:

I	will	ne	ver	blind	your	light	(seven)
nor	muf	fle	your	sounds of		love	(seven)
I	will	love	you	to	hea	ven	(seven)
I	swear it		gets	ea	si	er	

the doorsteps leading to your home were unwelcoming
how unwelcoming
(though you were so welcoming)
I wanted to cry wolf just so you could let me in
the beginning of fall was entirely evident
on those doorsteps

I vowed to only walk in
I know you have issues with people leaf-ing
so I brought you these flowers
without stems
in sevens
just for you

knock knock knots

I'm fidgeting
these panicked tulips
are staining my pockets
with all their jumping
and anxiety
and photosynthesis
and all the things nervous tulips do
in pockets
when they're about to break
such big news

and then your door opened

I forgot about the petals
pushing anxiously against my pelvis
and I just said it
I said it

I really said it

you smiled while
I fumbled with the sevens
of squished impressionable flowers
in my jeans
plucking them from the fabric
some folded or lightly torn
handing them to you
on the steps of your front door
mumbling
"but you can count them
please
count them
just to be sure"

· THE SEVENTEENTH ·

It was opening night
and my nerves
were free-falling
with charisma
and shame

in the middle of january
he was warm
it made sense

we were three months in love
that was enough
to want
to feel
more

he was gentle
though I wept in
his pillow
after
overwhelmed
with unfamiliar

it felt good
to give consent
for the first time

· NOSTALGIA *(STORYTELLING IN HAIKU)* ·

Daddy's magic hands
teach bunny ears on staircase
all from memory

even the leaves know
there is lesson in failure:
change color, wilt, fall

before we knew it
the bunnies skipped to high school
next to red hood wolves

'tis the season for
tall girl and short boy crushes—
the 'hoes' and 'hormones'

remembering when
bells ringing and belly rings
were synonymous

miss first period
to first missing period
a teen love affair

puberty, consent...
the infamous lack thereof
quickly girl learns worth

her memories tucked
behind frost and lunch money
time thaws the trauma

slow to rise for school
and yet quick to raise her voice;
queen misunderstood

parents hard at work
balance between filling void
and feeling freedom

life is a nightmare
never-ending dead-end dreams
the alarm clock sounds

because wake up calls
never catch you sleeping just
lying and awake

· DIAL TONE ·

He said
he didn't mind
not speaking to me
for a few days.
it didn't bother him.

> "well,
> when the heat
> awakens
> in your most
> shallow parts
> and it becomes
> convenient
> to love me again,
> I wouldn't mind
> missing your calls
> the way I used
> to miss us."

"c'mon, baby,
don't be so needy."

> "yeah, whatever."

· LOVE AS DECEIT ·

When saturday smelled like laundry,
candles and pit bull,
I knew I wasn't home
but I wanted so badly
for your place to be comforting.
something for me to get used to
for us.

it took seven years of laundry,
candles and pit bull
to realize
you were the acquired taste
my gut was so achingly
trying to reject.

· ANGELS ·

I had someone once and then I didn't have them anymore.
at sixteen, twenty and twenty-six,
all I was left with were my plans of who they might have been
and all the things I would have done
to bring security and happiness into our home.
but even those were eventually gone
when that thing happened in a cold october.
then again in a brutal august.
and again in a loveless february.
I have been emptied enough to have learned
the only thing that truly stays is the hollow.
I have had life expire inside of me enough to know
the rot it leaves behind.
am I chasing the sensation of feeling full
am I chasing refill
am I chasing rainbow baby— maybe
or maybe it was the rape months after the first miscarriage
that makes me crave something pretty after the rain
maybe it was the rape during the last miscarriage
that makes me not want to visit pittsburgh again
maybe this grief is too heavy to be held in my womb
maybe those motherfuckers are undeserving of my poem
maybe I just wanted the world to acknowledge my babies
maybe
maybe it's just easier for me to say I had someone once
but then I didn't have them anymore.

· PRELUDE ·

Battered
barred
bashed in
broken—
that's how being understood really feels.
like I've stolen from your thought pockets
and left you
baffled
bemused
and lint-less.

we're going to get personal.

· DEFLOWERED ·

Plundering deep
catching her bone on bait
hip-shift lateral
toward him
clothing forced to floor
body embezzled by hardwood
mouthful of rug
burnt tongue
bent arms behind back
back bruised
splintered stomach

"isn't this what you wanted?"

· INTERLUDE ·

To be frank, I've met several people I wouldn't want to meet again. I've suffocated in the presence of some that others would have smiled at. I've played protector at the cost of my mental health. I've returned to people who were my earthly hell. I've called the suicide hotline in a house full of people. I've made excuses for why I give myself 'less than' energy. I had to learn that I am deserving of the love I give to others. I had to learn that I am worth the trouble. I had to learn to love my past, present and future. I had to learn that self harm is an addiction. I had to learn to stop shutting down. I had to learn to stop feeling everything. I had to learn that emotions are not a light switch and it's up to me to figure out what my middle ground is. I went to therapy. I've faced karmic lessons where I had to consistently prove that I finally got it. that I finally understand.

there was a time when I was certain that I wouldn't write ever again.
I was certain that writing my trauma would make my book too heavy.
I didn't think that the world needed this—

I thought it would only bring down everyone's energy. but this is a testament to what healing (sometimes) looks like. consider this an interlude where I warn you that while yes, there is more to come, I would never emotional dump on you, drop the mic and call it poetry. we cannot regurgitate our pain and list out our trauma then applaud and move along. expression is only the first step. continue through the seasons. better is coming. but while you work toward better, please express gratitude for where you are now. be thankful for the places you have been delivered from. look forward to all the joys you have left to experience. because there's still so, so much joy left.

· AFTER SCHOOL ·

The television flashed cartoon on mute.

her back
sinking into sheet
beneath his mass
weighing on
and in her.

he was her supposed good friend back then.
she had spent years mapping out her identity
of what woman she would become.
come dusk, he became
the casketed shadows suffocating her eyelids
and tugging at her feet underneath the cloths
reminding her it just wasn't safe
enough
to be anyone.

his push shoved hers.
she heaved dust,
overcome by the gasps.
her back
sinking into sheet
beneath his mass
weighing on
and in her.

(her lungs were taught to breathe ember
but couldn't handle her ashes)

she quieted herself
to the swaying of his aching twin bed.
anxious for tears and coroner,
she tucked into her knees
when he was done.

"I thought you were urging me on."

she learned that 'no' meant 'yes'
when man is power hungry.

that fists in (his) chest
only encourage
the tightening of muscle.

how closing (her) eyes
makes time
tick
subtly
faster.

· DRAINED ·

I had been running for five months.

I didn't need any help
figuring it out.
didn't want any input
or advice
that I couldn't uphold.

but I would have liked water.

if someone had just given me water
then I could have kept running
for another
five months
(maybe figuring it out).

· POMPEII ·

I drew pictures on my arm last night
sierra leone loaned me 3d wounds:
distorted, disheveled and diamond-cut
beveled drops of blood
rose above my pivoted skin
pivoted
pivoted
palestinian skin
there's a jihad on my skin
remotely pivoting around blades

they say:
'didn't your mom ever tell you not to run with scissors?'

yes, these scissors are running across me
backtracking to safe havens and
searching for something recognizable
rocking
back and forth in solitude
with nothing but the rust from oxidized metal
to keep it company

I heard self-mutilation is a kid's game
with infantilized blades strong enough
to revert you back to innocence
and resurrect childhood through cell sacrifice

so last night I cut rape from yesteryear
this morning I was a child again
with calloused palms from hand bars
and sandy pebbles in my sneakers
ready for the abandonment of crippling sandbag baggage

I will orphan these memories at the foot of pompeii
beneath a cemetery of 20,000 decayed bodies
while sweeping after my footsteps in the volcanic ash

you said my body was an eruption
because of you all I see is the ashes
deep gashes and slashes now outline my cheekbone

slash   gash   slash   gash

each stroke more defined than the next
some slit wrists but I slit face in gill shapes carved in flesh
my manmade blinds kiss the sun before my lips can
they kiss my blood before you can strain the oxygen out of it

you call this unnatural beauty fucked up but   mothafucka
                                                      I'm
                                                      just
                                                      venting

and I don't mean venting like

      the vacant spaces encased in my ribcage
      you littered with guitar picks
      every time you plucked my bone marrow
      trying to tune
      my body to you
      because
      you are no sympathetic violinist

I'm venting like

      the secretion of blood copper pennies
      tucked in the hips
      of my wishbone legs
      every time you wished to bone
      poor fountain waters streamed away
      in tattered coats
      preferring to walk barefoot
      in sandstorm
      and lose themselves
      then play genie

you could never have me   by love
you could never have me   by choice

I'm venting like

      the rebirth of my womanhood
      when it sheds dead graffitied tissue
      after you tagged my vaginal walls
      like a harlem train station
      cause ain't nothin'
      renaissance
      about your art

see,
I drew pictures on my arm last night
x-acto blades carved a picasso in my skin
removing the rough draft of your sins
and now I can finger paint
with my crayolas
and magic markers

I am
a child again

three.

OUT OF SEASON

(these aren't the seeds I planted)

· MORNINGS AFTER ·

Here we are
loving each other without bones
skin full of soot and sun
limbs melting into one
to keep warm

these are the mornings we prayed for
heat awakening the honey between us like candied flesh
you assure me there's nothing hidden between us
(is it candid or finesse)
you tell me less is more
so I show up undressed
how 'bout you shed and molt your cloak
show me your depth
now who's asking who to strip

we outlasted the candles
and their blackened wicks
morning breath and breeze pushing the haze away

and there we laid
intertwined and spineless
bodies awkwardly forgetting exactly
how to be human

· IN HEAT ·

He softened me up
and I was his melted butter
but I never knew
if he was using me
because he was out of oil
or for my savory taste.

· THE ILLUSION OF WE, US AND OURS ·

This is the sound of a soul tie:
loving in syllables like small surges slowed down
for understanding (and to catch my grip)
sped up for entertainment (and the fun of the rough)
idling around equinox, 'not gonna happen' and never enough.
what is the last syllable I made you feel?
wet? numb?

I've used every 11:11 to wish for you;
unconcerned about the concept of time yet
still concerned about the conception of ours.

last I saw of you was at dinner
you've never been the type to let leftovers linger
always clearing the plate
clearing the table—
although that can be very disillusioning
if you have the tendency to overeat when you're satiated—
do I not fill you?
because I am sure there is someone
who will eat (me) and be filled.

baby, don't go wasting my time.

don't go wasting
good food.

· HUSH DIAMONDS ·

Remember that one summer you owed me apologies
but offered me carats?
when I would have let you off
for a fraction of the price
but you couldn't compromise pride
so you offered financial settlement instead?
then threatened to kill yourself if I didn't accept?

you have always been quite the negotiator.

quite the contractor—
contracting hits,
favors, sex deliveries.
such a prompt milkman.
your tagline should be:
"never out of work 'cause I'm always at your door."

you abused the sensitive side of me
but I refuse to be memorialized
for being subdued and vulnerable.
so I go gargoyle:
carved stone that cannot be
molded, manipulated, folded or shaped.

staying solid is the only thing I didn't change.

you told me be cool and to play my part
now I'm frostbitten; you're reminiscent
of when my heart was less sharp,
less locked,
more dependable,
more bendable.
but I'm comfortable.
comfortable and meditating in the darkness,
I reminisce on my innocence
once stolen from me by daylight.

you left me with a bad taste in my mouth.
and less money.

why does the woman in me have to suffer
for the girl you tried to take from me?
you sucked that little girl out of me.
I tried to throw her some rope
'cause I couldn't let her go.

I just could not   let   her   go.
so I   had to   let   her

                              hang.

· CEMETERIES ·

Why do victims always have to clean
after a monster's mess?

I don't remember burying all these bones,
oven hot urns
and tombstones.

I don't remember cradling carcass
and allowing it to envelop me
like extraskeletal skin.

· ALL IS FAIR IN LOVE AND WAR ·

The eye is the window to the soul and the calmest center of a storm
it is sweet enough to let you in but brutal after it moves on
'everyone says they love nature
until they realize how perilous she can be'
shipwrecked and lost in me
will make you a casualty to forget
I promise
droplets seep through my blinds but these blurs will not deter me
you thought you left me deserted
now sit in awe of me and my resilience

this is what it takes to keep my fire going:
engulfed in God, listening, head down in the trenches

you used your body to hurt me
your tongue slandered my name
I sat in stillness
with unwavering faith
he fuels my inferno 'cause I acknowledge his flame

you thought I walked the streets alone
knew I didn't have any brothers
but the thing about God is
he knows his way through the gutter
and nothing
goes unpunished

· SHOWERS ·

He described us as a quaint love
not quite ready for summer
yet full of enough wet to get us through.

the problem was he wanted me to come thru
without getting through
and I cannot see through all of these canopies.

is there more to you than seeing green?

with no love and no guarantees,
even the heat of our sultriest hour
will die down in the dismal dust of unrequited.
rainforests need love, too.
and I have a few rain showers eager to get to your root.

you say you want to play provider
but keep your truths tucked
like designated survivor
under code of conduct
rules about succession—
all you need to know is:
I come first then you come next.

but how you want me to irrigate your body
(of land) and I'm just getting settled?

our spirits naturally reject intruders
yet you lead me into your life
and leave me in labyrinth and illusion.
expecting me to appreciate the fantasy
of thinking I have you
while hiding my true jurisdiction.
treating me like bitch
with electric dog collar.
trying to pull a bait and switch—
I said I'm horny,
not stupid.
rain turned to mist
by the heat of the moment;
not even wet now I'm just hot, humid and fuming.
all because you stumble on questions like
'what are we doing?'

are you hiding a harem or are you just that indecisive?

because real ones can tell the truth
and still get what they want.
you're not taking the lead,
you're just leading me on.

· LOVE AND LIMB ·

Queen of cold feet but the warmest of hands
with a bosom soft enough for nestling;
tempted to come back for seconds
but never want to overstay my welcome.

how can our love marinate
if you eat me overnight?
do you want it freshly seasoned
or do you want it ripe?
if I let down the bridge for you
then what's the point of the moat?
if you cannot navigate deep waters
then how will you pour down my...
soul?

ready and ruminating on the phenomena of shortcuts,
only living once and somehow never getting old,
we let our impatience unfold;
negating our better judgment
we birthed a love
lacking quality
and control.

· POLLUTANTS ·

We were submerged in our own toxins
and somewhere beside each other
we became cancerous coma.

(maybe it is the emphysema keeping us together)

it is becoming
slightly impossible
to breathe
in here
but without
the stampede
I simply cannot
feel you.

(can we please address the elephants in the room?
they've been waiting and I don't know elephants to be patient)

I am becoming slightly protective
over this love junkyard we've created.
in fear of starting from scratch
we go thrifting.
when did our perception
of love start shifting
from sunflower field to landfill?

· ATTIC ANTIQUES ·

You left me with blank and void.
I don't want to replace the emptiness
we so carefully put together:
the gaps between my fingers
mimic shadows of yours
and when the sun isn't enough,
the moon illuminates its darkest corners.

but you fold me.

I am the origami in your forgotten pocket
next to the already chewed gum and grit
in your least favorite jeans
collecting dust like antique
and secondhand;
always second place
never vintage and well-aged
just aged and forsaken.
like yesterday's newspaper,
we were a quick statement that went mildly unnoticed.
eventful for the evening yet quiet in the morning.
our prints danced in the newsstands together
but your stories did not mention me.
all that time wasted on daily pages.

we could have made history.

· TABLE MANNERS ·

See,
I will always love you more
because your 'love'
is pure sugar
and will dissolve
in your dark waters
as quickly as it will take
those waters
to drown you.

keep your sugar.

I will not allow
for even your tiniest grains
to exfoliate and thin
my love
which remains
unprocessed, unrefined
and as raw as it comes.

keep your salt, too.

· ANCIENT CUPID AND MODERN HEARTBREAK ·

Them:
I wish we met later in this life.
I would've learned more
and put you through less.

me:
I wish we hadn't met at all.
if the arrow had better timing,
it would've been
a bullet
instead.

· HIS CHANEL ·

Unfamiliar fragrances fill the air like elephants
on the night he came home
smelling of perfidy and ivory.

his jaw clenched tight while sneaking in
then slowly released the moment
he thought he got away.

but oh,
how the fumes like to linger halfway
when they think they have
something to talk about.

· MUSCLE MEMORY ·

Muscle memory got my heart used to you;
passive aggression got you used to me
being used to you using me.

do not ask me to forget the nights
when the crickets were quieter than you—
when our memory foam mattress
couldn't remember
who you were.

the looms despise you.
you tiptoed on creaky hardwood
to disrupt the silence,
unthreading sheets unfamiliar to you
to become familiar with temples
you never believed in.

we were just bodies, where was your faith?

you set calamity to our calms
then rested our open hearts
in the cemetery you built
just for us.
maybe in this way we were special to you:
the man with such a big heart
and so much to give

who
would
he
have
been
had he not provided for the neighborhood matriarchy too?

do not ask me to forget the days
when the moon went to bed before you did.
while you were out stealing her warmth,
did you forget our long drives to open field
and stars together—
back when we thought we were happy?

muscle memory got my heart used to you,
but now I'm thinking that
my brain knows better.
next time you creep into another woman's walls
giving her something she can feel
to feel security in your manhood,
be considerate and consider
putting the ADT alarm on at least.

and please,
keep your diseases
to yourself.

· APERTURE ·

The blinds snitched on the morning
and they told me everything I needed to know.
peeking through the window,
it is ironic how high the red flags wave;
they either appear over your head or in your face,
but the aperture of your ignorance determines
whether they appear at all.

how much light do you want to let in?

I set the curtains on fire today.
left them burning in the fireplace on oak.
using the oxygen of our love, it chain-smoked.
now there are no more words
to provoke
to choke on
to lie with
to cry over
to deny speaking.
let the neighbors sightsee your treason
while this betrayal bonfire burns the maternal instinct in me
that always wants to protect you
despite you being disrespectful.

I listened to the sun come out one morning
and overheard her asking where I've been.

I've been underground and dirtied by sewage
underweight and feeling like nuisance
undervalued and overwhelmed by decision
under fire and doubting my position
underwater and drowning without guidance
misguided and largely underrated
under attack had to go undercover
can't crack 'cause my diamond's under pressure
had to get my thoughts under control
underdeveloped and highly overlooked
but over time my purpose is understood
stay focused and the blessings will unfold
the pain I undergo, I will overcome
underestimated and foolishly undermined
unbeknownst to them my harvest just takes time
undersoil my roots are underway
sprouting from my seeds underneath
grateful for grave 'cause now I'm planted deep
from spud to overgrown and making headway
they will say 'it happened overnight'

even though,
I only got slivers of sun
through the blinds.

how much light do you want to let in?

· BEST BY ·

When I am afraid and the moon is still,
and I am out of ear and dignity
but full of your apology—
is when I leave to take our dog
(and elephant) outside.

I spent most of the time shoveling:
grabbing the shovel
to dig out the rot
you have made of our 'us'.

today you are sorry
but tomorrow you'll want eggs.

you will have enough nerve to request dressings:
fresh spinach, grated swiss
and tomatoes.

and you think you've made an honorable woman out of me.

I was cleaner before I became one of your belongings;
I was cleaner (before your hands)
before I started belonging
in your hands
holding me up like lynch,
encasing me in book like god.

I am no one's to archive.

in one more moon
this shelf-life
will expire
and I will be out of here, baby.

and all you will have
left
of me
is this terrible taste
on the tip
of your tongue.

· KING OF HEARTS ·

You were too invested in my heart's elasticity
and finding its limits and bounds
to realize that it was never up
for sale,
auction,
foreclosure,
rent,
nor hire.

I cannot be discounted or lent.

but it was intriguing
watching
your love-shallow
cheap ass
try to negotiate
into nirvana.

· OWNERSHIP ·

I didn't want to be yours anymore, I wanted to be my own.
so I took the little girl in me to the park.
not because I wanted to play with her,
I just wanted to get away from you.
perfect example of a grown person
out looking for an excuse:
to leave, to fight, to invoke jealousy.
all these walls I've built surrounding me
to keep you out
actually kept me in.
I tried to escape you and could only find me.
but I didn't know me so I only saw you.
still caught up on you,
I lost the chance to learn me.
I abandoned myself;
dropped me off at someone else's house
promising to come back without looking back.
made promises to myself that I coulda, shoulda, woulda kept.
promises that I wouldn't think twice to break
if only they were made
to someone else.

I used to tell you about yourself
and your fear of being intimate (still true).
standing in the mirror it's evident the feeling's mutual—
my problem is being self-committed.

the greatest gift one can offer themselves is loyalty.
without it, survival of the fittest will win
every time.
and there is no prize for self-sacrifice
and martyr
and if there was—
would you really be willing to lose life
just to barter for a lengthier wikipedia page?
at least bargain for something more concrete.
you always have more control than you think,
if you just think.
things are never as bad as they seem.
even the hate train eventually loses steam.

so yeah,
I didn't want to be yours anymore.
I wanted to be my own.
and regardless of how I got here,
the lesson has been learned.
and as far as doubling back
that's a direction I no longer turn.

· TAKIN' OUR 'P' WORD BACK ·

Woman,
you lie on your back
in grass
using abacus
to count the moons they missed.

do not let them steal your summer solstice.

you were imported from ossuary
because your good flesh
is stronger
than any boning
man could use to define you.

leave those skeletons alone.

and if your sun plateaus mid-horizon:
lower the valley to heighten the hill.

your womb is earth's axle.
let your blood break ground,
light fire and go phoenix.

put your pussy in perspective.

four.

FOR HARVEST
BY SUMMER
(taking stock)

· I SOLEMNLY SWEAR YOU HAVE ME F'D UP ·

I gave you honesty
when you wanted flattery
and I just cannot fathom feeling sorry
for not feeding your deflated ego.

and I am certainly not sorry you're frustrated
because you foolishly believed I would
compromise self,
compromise health,
compromise morals over you.

I am not sorry
for my 'bad timing' of cutting ties
though I'm not sure what you expected.
the regrets become expensive
when you nickel and dime every problem.

the dissolution of our union is not what I wanted,
but I am not sorry you did not spend enough
nipple time with mother
or 'man talk' with father
or whichever excuse you want to use this week
for your inability to show up on time
to be loved.

and while I do apologize for evacuating
(all) the tissue paper from our place,
I am not sorry for vacating said space
without notice
'cause when your ego began
to crowd our apartment,
crowd our chakras
and crowd our kitchen—
fucking up the savory sensations
of my oxtail—

I just knew something had to give.

· WHOLE FOODS ·

Adulthood (womanhood) (manhood)
does not begin when blown raspberries
on your stomach as a kid are replaced
by other fruit and toppings.

it begins underground when you connect to the root,
center energy in earth and grow whole.

wholeness is not an extension of you.
wholeness is not outside of you.
wholeness is not found in your 'better' half.

in your body, you are home.
in your body, you belong.
in your body, you are complete.

I know it's tempting to leave your bones behind
to be buried in someone else,
but you aren't the kind of flower we leave at graveyards.
this isn't the plot written and dug for you.
you didn't travel from seed to never see sun.
you were reserved for the living.
you deserve pleasure, the thrill.
just remain rooted in hole,
rooted and whole.

· HUMAN HUMUS ·

He used the thought
of me to scent his home
like potpourri,
only I
wasn't his dying flower,
I was composting myself
for the garden
of a worthier man.

· PLEASE EXCUSE THE BASS IN MY FEMININE VOICE ·

I don't want to be remembered as weak
yes, my bosom is delicate
my blossom is delicate
I don't mind 'delicate'
but do not misinterpret
my womanhood as powerless
the idea that I am 'too fragile' to play with
or that I am fragile enough
to play with

I am already perceived
as dandelion
within a patriarchal garden:
beautiful, nutritious, holistic
but still a weed

I cannot afford to be anything
besides guerrilla

· LOVING SELF ·

Too often do we make competition out of living.

it is not about who is better,
it is knowing you
are not less.

quite frankly,
I am too critical of myself
to be competing
with anyone.

· FALUMA (REST IN POWER SISA AGI) ·

I woke up black, unbothered and supernatural
mind switching like hips
in laterals
changing direction
swiftly
away from you

feet following the leader
(the soca)
I stepped on balcony
spreading my linens on laundry day
one baby step away
from hovering untied in the air
black girl sorceress
envision me
wrapped in my cotton sheet
floating like doves do

faluma ding ding ding!

watching from sky as their hands
prepare poison for me
to drink
trying to kill all this black girl magic
my eyes full of startle at the task

I wonder what kind of hands
you must have
to feel threatened
by little ol' me

faluma ding ding ding!

maybe it was the glare
from the horizon beneath my feet
that made my stomping
and waving
and twisting constellations
all the more phenomenal
or their stares as they
gazed at me like planetarium
as my dance made their hairs
stand from the follicle
another mission failed
they left entranced
in my waters
while I remained
untouched
black
supernatural
and unbothered

· IN HER LANGUAGE ·

She is no one's thirty second commercial.
she does not sell her virtue like product
purposely using popular poses and phrases
to get your blood rushing.

she is more than a moment.
more satisfactory than instant gratification,
quick fix and affectionate transactions.

she is well traveled,
always arriving well dressed,
and if she wants to be read from

                                                                right

                                to

left

you had better convert
and master her language
as if it's your first
as if it's vernacular
as if you taste her worth
and only seek to empower her
with each spread
of your tongue.

· BLACK TEA AND BACKACHES ·

At least I have
my books
my pens
my incense
my 'I got this'
my crown
my acrylics
my supple hips
and slow reggae dancin'
my prayers
my peace
my place
my voice
my integrity
my honor
my ancestry
my choice

there is no bad attitude
that my gratitude cannot reverse

· LOVE EDUCATION ·

Owning fault:
not your mama's
not your daddy's
not society's
yours

learned behaviors:
reciprocity
communication
putting yourself first

don't go jumping:
from balcony
to conclusions
into relationship
(doing these may lead back to balcony)

· DÉJÀ VU ·

My eyes stared beyond the mast.
we were limp stalks in the sun
nestling in calloused fragments
beneath airy blanket and linen.

this feels familiar.

not because I think we're soul mates,
I've just been through this before:
the casualness of the sailing soul
and the casualty of a soul celled.

we did it in the rough of spring.
not so delicately,
not so in love,
but we were honest about it.
about liking each other
for the (t)horny,
deflowered stems we were.

· BUTTERFLIES ·

I just want you to know it's okay if it hurts.

if you touch me and my skin ripens with all those tiny bumps.

if you rub me and (all) the butterflies escape
overwhelmed and overcrowded
in the new york of my womb,
the high rise of my summer solstice.
or if your body temperature
isn't as pleasant as I had wanted
because I am aware defrosting takes time.

it's okay if your elders' eyebrows rise
as they sneer at the ambers and browns
of my incandescent feathers,
because they grew up in an era
when black people were only allowed
to have skin.

oftentimes what you ask for
may not come in the package you envision,
but I promise
this is what being in right love feels like.

· WHEN LOVE MOVES IN ·

You are
consuming my mind
compromising my breath
challenging my longing
cultivating my song

you are more rehab
than you are trigger

you are more.

· HEARTWARMING ·

I thought my cardiac caverns were soundproof
until your eardrums beat to the same rhythm.

you heard my heart beat even when its valves were closed.

your being is warmth
and I will forever be drawn
to your origami and confetti-papered heat.

may the forest fire spread quickly.

· TOOTSIE POP ·

How many men will it take to get to him
(my king charming) and will he mind
the many men in my rearview mirror
hollerin' at their sweet suckle daisy to c'mon back
tryin' to coo me through their phones and to their beds
after I already done got in love and comfortable

will he still love me
when he understands the magnitude
of his woman being vulnerable
when he sees the kinds of men I've loved
(who did not necessarily love back)
coming back for seconds
not that all of them had a sexual sampling
just that they all thought they owned me
and want return on their investment

will it matter the rape it took
the ache it took
the slit wrists and attempts
or will he only count
the licks

· LOAVES ·

Once upon a time,
there was a little girl who would dream of you.
you were a little boy and too many hopscotches away for her to reach,
but she prayed you would find your way to her.
she promised she would save herself for you and only you.
but that was before she found out promises weren't sealed like spells—
before she found out they were merely words whose magic
lay within the lips of the speaker.
that little girl sure did try to keep her promises.

as a young lady,
every time she thought she found you, she left crumbs of herself.
the amount of crumbs left with those other young men
(counterfeit copies of the youthful you)
signified their love for her.
in their quantity, they represented her willingness to return.
some of her crumbs were stolen.
some were wasted.
some came up missing.
some remain unaccounted for
on account of those momentary moments
where she would stop counting, counting crumbs.
you were the one—
the one infinity she saved her crumbs for.

but her loaf ran out.

her temple is looking for the body of christ
to begin the holy communion
but there is no bread.
yet every time you two met,
she left you thousands of crumbs (about half of her loaf)
and you hung onto them faithfully without speaking any oaths.
it was as though your souls made the promises for you.

there is a woman who dreams of you.
you see a good god in her but is her 'good' god enough?
her presence reminds you god is but is there enough god within you?
will you keep vows and be honorable?
I wonder
does it bother you
that she was walkin' around
unconsciously spendin' half your bread?
or do understand that you can rebuild her god
from the half you kept?
give a woman god and the god will never leave.
that's how you get your master peace.

once upon a time,
there was a little girl who dreamt of you.
she grew into a young lady who had the pleasure of meeting you.
she became a woman who is now needing you—
to knead her.

· THINGS ·

The sun walked off the earth this evening
like we gave her something to be mad about

and we had nothing to be ashamed of

the sand danced beneath the heat of us:
we were intoxicated with creation
having spent our day
mounted in earth and dirt
digging deep and sowing

sure enough I am unsure of where this is going

certain only of my desires:
I want to be surrounded by your stuff
crowd your space and feel you

we can dance all night if you want to
we can lay together like plants
using only our intimacy to photosynthesize
(we will deal with the sun in the morning)
but this evening I just want us
to feel what it's like
to blossom
over and over
again

· OIL AND OCEAN ·

There is a thing to be said about how people treat you
utter discomfort is not love

when love fulfills you
when it replenishes the liters of water it wrung from your feet
when it presses almonds in bucket to wax on your bones
when the love is so grounded it wills wild marjoram to rise up from it
that is when you must call it unto your home
bring it inland and tuck it into your vale
for safekeeping

only you can decide what love looks like, acts like and is
at times it may be surprising, confusing and difficult
but it should never feel as though you must gut yourself
and be filled only with them
to keep it alive

love will ask and require you to grow
but it would never ask you
to decompose

· BRAILLE ·

For the women in braille
tired of being felt
tired of being told they were asking for it
tired of possessive proprietors
being part of them
like peninsula
tired of missing membrane
supposed to protect them
but never present
tired of pried open
tired of too friendly neighbors
tired of sharing space
tired of collecting rainwater
with pail
for kettle
to steam clean
the red
off bedding
after too friendly neighbor
pries
them open
though no one
believes them
because they were
walking braille
asking to be felt

for the men in mime
ashamed and sunken in silence
ashamed that it happened to them
ashamed to admit it happened at all
whether too ashamed to talk
or shamed into keeping quiet
causing their tongues
to tie and riot
to rip and rot
storytelling through gloved hands
and suppressive box
and panicked gestures
that look emphatic and entertaining
the audience claps
while they're ashamed and emasculated
weighed down by stigma
ashamed to have been felt
using sign language to be heard
and poems like these
that speak their stories through me
like ventriloquist
to remind us that a monsters' hit list
is not gender explicit
age specific
or past history
and family tie considerate

for the boys who became men and the girls who became women
scared of hands and kisses
scared of intimate moments
no matter how brief and innocent
scared to hug their sons
and love them like mothers
scared to open up to their children
and love them like fathers
because of how quickly touch can imitate smother
and suffocation
and things being taken and stolen
scared of the monsters
in their faces
in their friends
in their bodies
in the shadows and in the open
scared of becoming a monster themselves
for the people who were once victims and are healing from their hells
WE WILL ERUPT LIKE A PLAGUE POMPEII
TO LEAVE THESE MONSTERS IN FAMINE ALONE
TO STARVE THEM OF THE PEOPLE WE ONCE WERE
TO REINCARNATE THE DREAMS, THE PEACE
AND INNOCENCE WE ONCE HAD
TO WALK ON WET CONCRETE WITHOUT APOLOGY
WITHOUT NEEDING YOURS
AND WITHOUT HAVING TO TAKE IT BY FORCE

· DEAR SURVIVOR ·

You are not responsible
for having to find an explanation
for the pain someone caused you.
trust that you are worth being explained
every last detail to,
but if they had known your worth,
there would be nothing to search for.

please do not compromise your well-being
by trying to find and create answers.

· SUNGODS ·

In this darkened, damp asphalt alley of solitude,
women were sparking like matches or witches;
rubbing together like sticks
and branch switches.
from bird's view,
they were a light post congregation
swaying in concrete stew.
every second,
light would emerge
through a dimmed head of hair,
and surprisingly, men were there.
they were as present as gods.
moving like the women's shadows,
moving in throngs.
and it was their support
that helped keep the lights on.
see, all of these women were daughters,
but the men treated them
like suns.

· FULL CIRCLE ·

Strength is
consistency in self
when it is far easier
to come out of character.

it is being given nothing you need
and still showing up
on time for your dissilience.

it is sitting on stoop sifting through
hurt upon hardship and still budding
from bodega-seasoned sunflower seeds.

it is converting all odds to your side
and teaching them reciprocity.

· ABOUT THE AUTHOR ·

Sonia Summer, pseudonym of Allison Elizabeth White, is a first generation American writer from Long Island, New York. She taught High School Television Production for seven years in Prince George's County, Maryland. She received her Masters of Education in Curriculum & Instruction at Concordia University-Nebraska.

Summer is the last born of her loving Jamaican parents. Her pen name honors her mother whose support allowed her to frequent open mics and slam poetry competitions throughout New York City as a teen. She chooses to navigate her experiences through the lenses of spoken word, poetry, short stories and video production. She is dedicated to serving others and mentoring them to also speak their truths in healthy, meaningful ways. *Sunflower Seeds* is her first published book.

For more Sonia Summer, use the QR code below to get the most up-to-date information or visit www.soniasummer.com.

· FINAL REMARKS ·

For my alpha and omega—
I used to hesitate to express my love for God.
now I simply cannot leave God out.
in the most inclusive, nonjudgmental way possible,
I hope these words may carry you as they have done for me:

"For I know the plans I have for you," declares the Lord,
"plans to prosper you and not to harm you,
plans to give you hope and a future."
Jeremiah 29:11

and for when times are exceptionally hard
and you are considering leaving,
please stay:
call 9-8-8 (US)

Made in the USA
Middletown, DE
28 September 2022